ISBN 13: 979-8614-791735

Addiction is a disease that effects every part of a person, including the relationships they have with children. This book is intended for use by families, foster families, and counselors to help children and teenagers understand drug and alcohol dependency. This book is for minors that are in full contact, visitations, occasional phone calls, or fully removed from a parent with drug dependency. Children of drug dependent parents most often feel unloved, unimportant, and helpless. Part of healing for children and teens is coming to terms through understanding how drug dependency effects their parent. This book teaches that even though drug dependency changes many parts to a person, including their ability to care for themselves, underneath the dependency the parent loves the child.

This book is intended as a tool to open conversation about a parent's dependency problems. Not every child is ready to know the full details of their parent's drug dependency. The potential benefits and costs to opening the discussion should be carefully decided by those caring for the minor. This book is very comprehensive but it is impossible to cover every facet of a child's interactions or thoughts about a parent with a drug dependency problem. The book encourages talking openly and freely with trusted adults about thoughts and feelings related to a parent's dependency.

This book is intentionally written without a clearly defined ending for the child or parent. This is because for many children there is not ever an exact end point to addiction. The parent has to be on guard to avoid relapse and children may have fears of abandonment, resentment, or grief for the missed years together. The point of this book is to be read together. This opens up conversation in a positive way about a parent's drug or alcohol dependency which will allow for an exchange about the future for their parent and themselves.

Everyone wants our children to grow up feeling safe and loved. To build resiliency in a child means we must be able to show our children we, as adults, can handle strong feelings. By using this book, children learn that we can handle strong feelings by being open to talk about them, rather than suppressing them in fear. Children are constantly trying to make sense of the world around them. This book shows them a view of dependency that makes sense to them and instills the view that they are loved, capable, and important.

Every family is different. There is no family like yours. Sometimes a family has a parent, like a Mom or Dad, that is with you. They take care of you, talk with you, and spend time with you.

Just like Alex and his Dad.

Sometimes a parent has to take care of other important things too, like a Dad who is also a soldier has to go help out at another place or country. A Mom who is also a doctor has to take care of someone who is sick at a hospital.
Alex's Dad is a mechanic. He fixes cars that are broken.

When your parent is away from you, they still care about you because you are so important. It is Dad's job to fix cars that break down. When he is taking care of broken cars, Alex's Dad has to be gone for a long time.

Sometimes a parent has to be away from you for a long long long time. When they are gone, your parent has people care for you. Alex is part of this family because Alex's Dad wants to make sure Alex is taken care of while he is taking care of broken cars.

A parent loves you but has to care for other things too.
You are still important to your parent when they are not
there. Dad has to take care of the broken cars, himself,
and Alex. Dad cannot be with Alex as much as he wants
to be there but Alex is still taken care of.

Sometimes a parent has to take care of themselves first before being with you. Some parents have a sickness, illness, or disease called addiction. Addiction is a sickness. Addiction means they sometimes are not themselves. Addiction is a sickness where a person is stuck doing drugs or drinking an alcoholic drink.

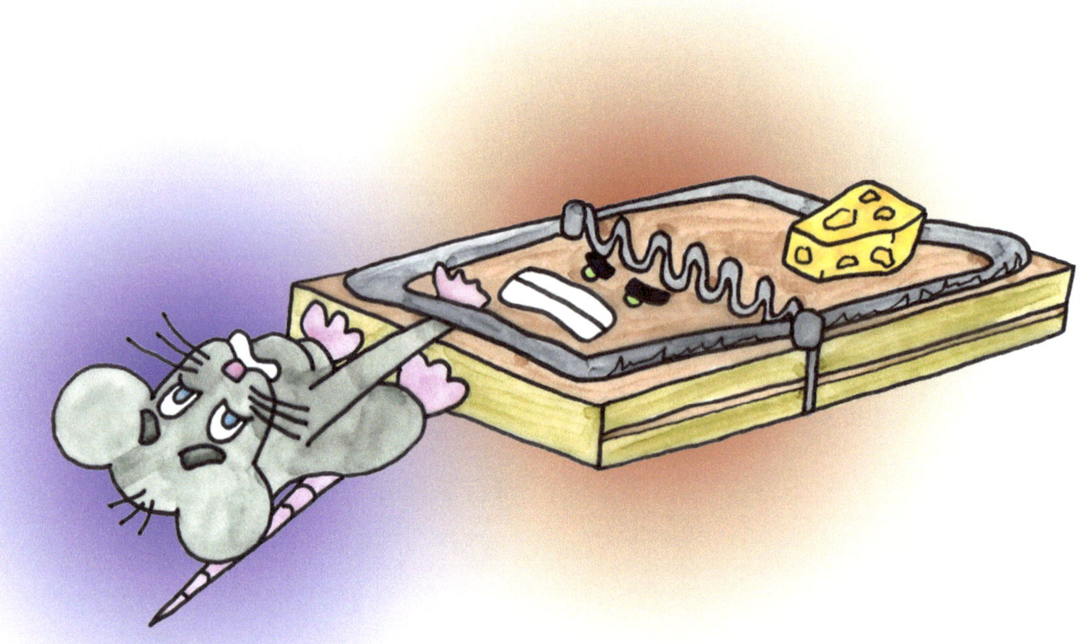

Drugs and alcohol are like a trap for those with addiction. A trap can get an animal stuck where they cannot get free to do things they want to do.

Drugs and alcoholic drinks can be like a trap that can get a parent stuck. Then the parent is not free to do the things they want to do.

When a person is sick, they do not mean to act the way they do. When you get sick you may feel tired or throw up even though you do not want to. You do not have control over what you do when you are sick. When a parent has the sickness of addiction from a drug or alcoholic drink, they may also do things they do not want to do. It is like their body is taken over by the disease.

When a parent has the illness of addiction, they may be really mean or scary even if they do not want to. They may say scary and confusing things. The parent might not even remember things that happened, even big things that they did, like hurting someone or threatening someone. The parent may do mean and violent things when they are sick with addiction.

When a parent is sick with addiction, they might blame others for bad things. The parent might say someone did things the wrong way, even if they did it the right way or the way they asked. The parent may say to do things a certain way but then be upset when they are done the way they said to do them.

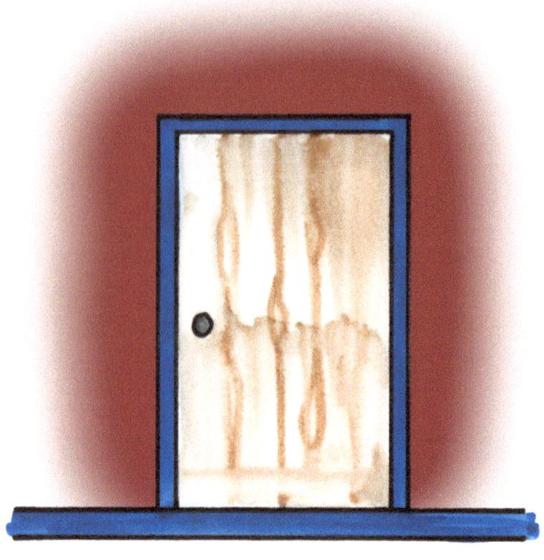

Sometimes addiction can make the parent do nothing at all. Not even get out of bed or talk with anyone. They might lock themselves in a room and not let anyone in. They might never ever leave the home, or the opposite and not come back home.

It is like the addiction has taken over the parent's body. Part of the sickness of addiction is also that the parent does not want to talk about it or they get mad if someone says something about the addiction.

The sickness makes them try to hide the addiction.
The disease makes them lie about it or ask others to lie about it.
They tell people lies about what they are doing.

It is like they are a whole different person when they are sick and confused by addiction.

When the sickness of addiction takes over a parent's body, a child might feel scared, confused, worried, and want to get away. Sometimes the child wants to take the place of the parent and do everything for them. The child might try to throw out or hide all the alcohol and drugs. The child may even feel responsible for the parent and want to take care of the parent, hide their keys, and get them healthy again. This never works for long.

Sometimes a child thinks, "I am the only one that can take care of him." The sickness of addiction cannot be fixed by a child. It is not a kid's job to take care of the parent. Only adults can help with addiction just like only surgeons can help do surgery. Alex is not with his Dad because Alex's Dad is sick with an addiction to drugs and alcoholic drinks.

Alex feels like he has two different Dads in the same body.

One Dad does not drink or do drugs and they can have really good times together.
One Dad does drink and he is a completely different person.

Alex knows which Dad is in control of his body because of the smells, how he acts different, or how his Dad's feelings get really big.

The disease of addiction does not start like other sickness. It is not something that spreads from person to person like a cough or a cold. Addiction starts like pushing over bigger and bigger dominos. Once an adult starts drinking an alcoholic drink or doing drugs, it will keep going until it pushes down everything and everyone. Sometimes a child feels blamed for someone else's addiction but it is not the child's fault. Alex's Dad has one alcoholic drink and it becomes more and more and more.

The disease of addiction is not like some other sicknesses. A cold might make someone sick for only a few days. The flu might make someone sick for a week. A broken bone might take even longer, a few months to be better. The disease of addiction takes a long long long time to be better. Alex's Dad wants to be with Alex but the disease keeps him away. Addiction with parents can change them on the inside of their mind and make them think they want more.

Sometimes parents cannot be with you because they need to take care of other things, like themselves and their sickness of addiction. Sometimes Dad might never call. Dad never comes to visit Alex because his Dad has to find a way to be healthy again with the help of other adults. Right now, Dad is sick and confused from the addiction disease. Dad's disease thinks he does not want to be with Alex. It will take Dad a long long long time to find a way to think clearly and be healthy again.

Alex's Dad is like a whole different person when he is sick with addiction. There is his Dad and there is his sick Dad. His Dad loves to be with Alex and do fun things together. Alex's sick Dad is not fun to be around and Alex is not being taken care of by his Dad. When Alex's Dad is sick with addiction, his Dad cannot take care of Alex but he still wants Alex to be taken good care of by someone who can care for him.

Sometimes when a parent is trying to recover and get better from the sickness of addiction, they might call or visit. Sometimes a parent cannot call or visit because the addiction tells them not to. A parent wants to call but the addiction traps them by changing their thinking and by changing what they want.

Because Dad wants to have Alex taken good care of, Dad has a family take care of Alex. Alex obeys and is nice while his Dad is not there. While Alex is getting taken care of, his Dad is trying to take care of himself and get rid of his sickness.

When Alex is waiting for his Dad to think clearly and be healthy again, Alex can still have fun and be kind to his family, friends, teachers, and those around him. While Alex is waiting he still has good people that care about him right now.

It is okay for Alex to be sad or to think about his parent that is gone right now. It helps Alex to feel better when he talks with someone about how he is feeling or how he misses his Dad. He talks about how he feels in his body. Sometimes Alex wants to cry because he misses his Dad and feels alone or abandoned even though he is with someone right now. Sometimes Alex wants to yell and scream because he is angry with his Dad. Sometimes Alex would feel guilty even though he was not doing anything bad at all. Alex wants his Dad to not have the disease of addiction and to spend time together with him. Alex tells his family how he is feeling and it helps him feel better.

Alex does things to make him feel better for a while like drawing, breathing slowly, cooking, writing nice things about himself or others, watching movies with friends, playing a musical instrument, or listening to good music. These things help Alex for a while but talking with someone he can trust about how he feels about his Dad helps him a lot more.

Alex can play, learn, make friends, follow directions, help others, be honest, and have fun even when his Dad is not there. Alex is a kid and he has people around him that care for him and want him to be happy. Alex's Dad is not there to help Alex or watch him grow up because of his sickness of addiction. Alex knows he is still important to his Dad because his Dad helped him by making sure Alex is being taken care of right now.

Common Questions

In order of maturity, some common questions or things to be prepared for if choosing to begin opening conversation about a parent's dependency include:

1) Are they ever going to get better?
2) Why can't they stop?
3) Do they care more about the drugs/alcohol than me?
4) When are they coming back/visiting again?
5) Are medications and drugs the same thing?
6) What can make them get better?
7) Do I have to take care of them or help make them better?
8) Is it okay to feel angry (or other emotion) at them?
9) Is it my fault?
10) Why don't they call/visit?
11) How come they cannot spend more time with me?
12) Why do they use drugs/alcohol?
13) What is it like to use drugs?
14) Why do they get so mad, sad, or confused sometimes?
15) Have you ever used drugs?
16) Why does it take so long to get better?
17) Why can't I "fix" them?
18) Do they have to hit "rock bottom" first to get better?
19) How come some people can drink alcohol and be fine but some people cannot?
20) Why do they say they do not love me?
21) What does it mean to be an enabler?
22) What is rehab?
23) What is relapse?
24) What is an AA/NA group?
25) Are they even trying to be better?

See these other therapy books by Leo DeBroeck, LMHC, CMHS

When Dad Got Scared: A child's guide to adult after trauma- A story for young children to better understand how trauma effects parents and adults that are close to them.

Grandpa's Circle- A story about learning to accept grief and loss by holding onto positive memories about the dead.

The New Normal: Life after abuse and neglect- A story about learning how life and change can be hard after parent abuse or neglect.